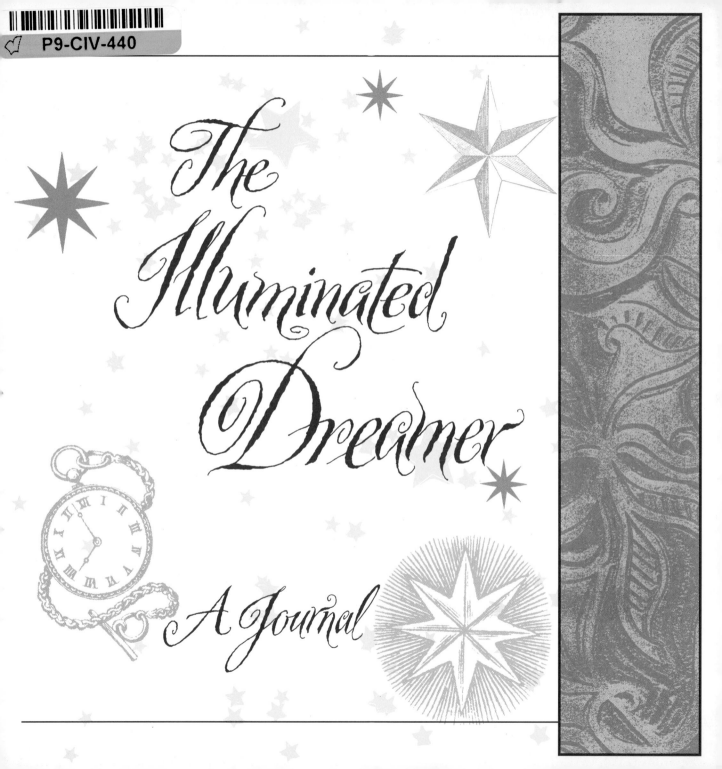

The Illuminated Dreamer

A Journal

First published in 1995 by
Collins Publishers San Francisco
1160 Battery Street
San Francisco, CA 94111-1213

A Packaged Goods Incorporated Book

Conceived and produced by
Packaged Goods Incorporated
276 Fifth Avenue, New York, NY 10001
A Quarto Company

Designer: Carol Malcolm Russo / Signet M Design, Inc.
Cover Calligraphy: Anita Karl
Editor: Kristen Schilo
Production Manager: Tatiana Ginsberg

ISBN: 0-00-225110-8

Color Separations by Wellmak Printing Press Limited
Printed and bound in Hong Kong by Sing Cheong Printing Co., Ltd.

CollinsPublishersSanFrancisco
A Division of HarperCollins*Publishers*

DATE

_____

TIME

_____

D A T E

_____

T I M E

_____

There was a time when

meadow, grove,

and stream,

The earth, and every

common sight,

To me did seem

Apparelled in

celestial light,

The glory and the

freshness of a dream.

WILLIAM
WORDSWORTH

From the fixed place of

heaven she saw

Time like a pulse

shake fierce

Through all the worlds,

Her gaze still strove

Within the gulf to pierce

Its path; and now she

spoke as when

The stars sang in

their spheres.

D A N T E
G A B R I E L
R O S S E T T I

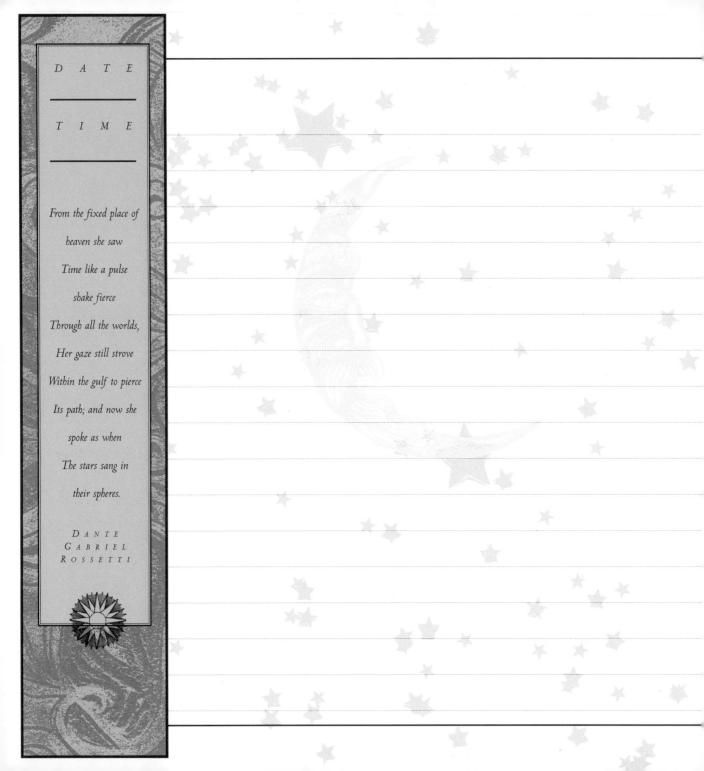

DATE

TIME

DATE

_____

TIME

_____

_____

Over his keys the musing
organist,
Beginning doubtfully and
far away,
First lets his fingers
wander as they list,
And builds a bridge from
Dreamland for his lay:
Then, as the touch of his
loved instrument
Gives hope and fervor,
nearer draws his theme,
First guessed by faint
auroral flushes sent
Along the wavering vista
of his dream.

J A M E S
R U S S E L
L O W E L L

DATE

————————

TIME

————————

How sweet the moonlight

sleeps upon this bank!

Here will we sit, and let

the sound of music

Creep in our ears: soft

stillness, and the night,

Become the touches of

sweet harmony.

W I L L I A M
S H A K E S P E A R E

DATE
————

TIME
————

DATE

———————

TIME

———————

DATE

TIME

*Inside the light
your soul makes
its circle,
refining itself to
extinction,
or enlarging its rings
like the stroke of
a bell.*

PABLO
NERUDA

DATE

—————

TIME

—————

. . . her eyelids trace maps

of strange geographies,

savage tattoos kept only

in the tenuous

circle of her dreams.

*MARJORIE
AGOSIN*

DATE

TIME

D A T E

_____

T I M E

_____

The sun is hot like wine

And the moon is cool

like a cup;

Pour the sun

into the moon.

The face of love

Can only be seen

in dreams;

Pour me the cure

which brings sleep.

V I N C E N Z O
D A V I C O

DATE

TIME

. . . in her 98 years

to discover

8 comets

She whom the moon ruled

like us

levitating into the night sky

riding the polished tenses.

A D R I E N N E
R I C H

DATE

TIME

DATE

TIME

Love lies in sleep,

The happiness of

healthy dreams:

Eve's dews may weep,

But love delightful seems.

JOHN CLARE

DATE

TIME

Swiftly walk o'er the
western wave,
Spirit of Night!
Out of the misty
eastern cave,
Where, all the long and
lone daylight,
Thou wovest dreams
of joy and fear,
Which make thee terrible
and dear,
Swift by thy flight!

PERCY
BYSSHE
SHELLEY

DATE

TIME

DATE

_____

TIME

_____

Even sleepers

are workers and

collaborators

in what

goes on

in the universe.

HERACLITUS

DATE

TIME

What I do

And what I dream

include thee,

as the wine

Must taste of its

own grapes.

E L I Z A B E T H
B A R R E T T
B R O W N I N G

Which through the sky

draw Venus' silver team;

For sure they did not seem

To be begot of any

earthly seed,

But rather angels, or of

angels' breed . . .

E D M U N D
S P E N S E R

A poem should be wordless
As the flight of birds.

A poem should be
motionless in time
As the moon climbs,

Leaving, as the moon
releases
Twig by twig the
night-entangled trees,

Leaving, as the moon
behind the winter leaves,
Memory by memory
the mind——

A poem should be
motionless in time
As the moon climbs.

A R C H I B A L D
M A C L E I S H

DATE

TIME

Sunset and evening star,
And one clear call for me!
And may there be no
moaning of the bar,
When I put out to sea,
But such a tide as moving
seems asleep,
Too full for sound
and foam,
When that which drew
from out the
boundless deep
Turns again home.

A L F R E D ,
L O R D
T E N N Y S O N

DATE
_____

TIME
_____

The moving Moon went

up the sky,

And nowhere did abide;

Softly she was going up,

And a star or two beside~

SAMUEL
TAYLOR
COLERIDGE

Once upon a midnight dreary, while I pondered, weak and weary,
Over many a quaint and curious volume of forgotten lore,
While I nodded, nearly napping, suddenly there came a tapping.
As of some one gently rapping, rapping at my chamber door.
" 'Tis some visitor," I muttered, "tapping at my chamber door—
Only this, and nothing more."

E D G A R
A L L A N P O E

DATE

TIME

DATE

_____

TIME

_____

Every hour, every moment
has its specific
attendant Spirit;
the clock-hand, minute
by minute,
ticks round its
prescribed orbit;
but this curious
mechanical perfection
should not separate but
relate rather,
our life, this
temporary eclipse
to that other . . .

H.D.
(HILDA
DOOLITTLE)

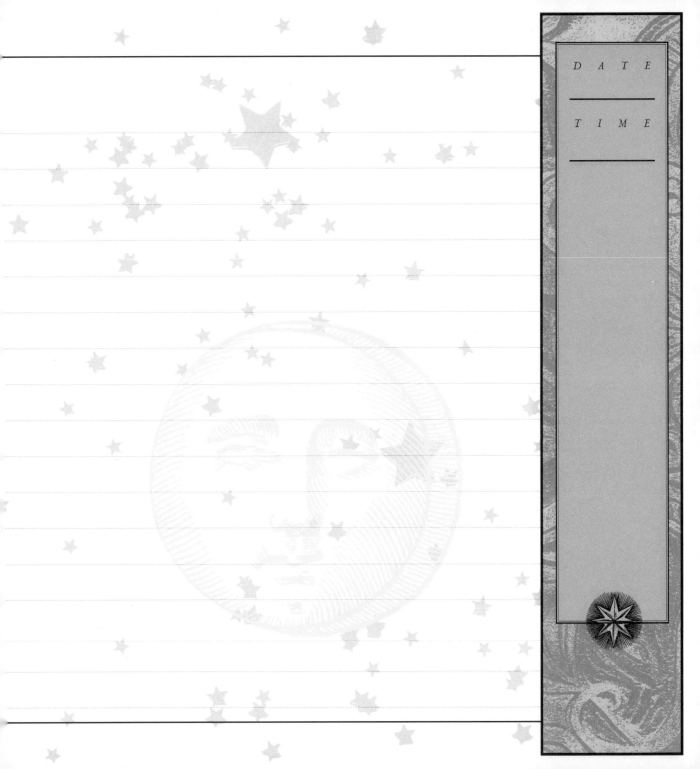

Rose, oh pure contradiction,

joy of being

No-one's sleep

under so many lids.

R A I N E R
M A R I A
R I L K E

*Her eyes were open, but
she still beheld,
Now wide awake, the
vision of her sleep:
There was a painful
change, that nigh expelled
The blisses of her dream
so pure and deep . . .*

J O H N   K E A T S

Traveler repose and dream

among my leaves.

W I L L I A M
B L A K E

DATE

———————

TIME

DREAM THEMES

DREAM THEMES

DREAM THEMES